As I read Lance Newman's proverbial poems, a
fragile cabin of existential questions built itself in my mind: "What /
follows from what I know?" "Am I equal to / the awakened life?" These
beautiful Thoreauvian meditations are remedy to the "machines of
doubt" our time's getters and spenders have placed like bombs in the
palms of our hands.

   Jennifer Moxley

"Truth is as constant as work," Lance Newman says
in one of his *Proverbs of Earth*—and only so constant, I think as I
read the poems, impersonal in their first-person and often gnomic
voice. This is a book I carry with me, pick up and lay down and pick
up again, interested in the rhythm of breath and the stripped-down
statement—or, on another reading, that I follow all the way through
its meditations on weather, deep time and domesticity (the same, the
poems tell me), the work of books, the growing and taking of food,
the body as its own animal, money. I don't know until later that the
poems have made an argument, a compelling one, about how to live.

   Katharine Coles

Proverbs of Earth **is Lance Newman's** hand-made mix
tape of *Walden*: a deep dive into language with fresh takes on some
very American ideas. These poems give us a cigarette break from
capitalism, helping us think in a place and time that just wants us
distracted and a little pissed off. Lines and sentences in these quiet
protest poems can feel like Jenny Holzer's truisms: "One life is a snare/
and one a winter cottage"; "I try to be content/but I'd rather preach

fire"; "I learned/better than to mortgage/my work to a broker's taste"; "What if we refused/to burn dollars for fuel?" "Am I equal to/an awakened life?" *Proverbs of Earth* is a Magic 8-Ball, a Thoreauvian oracle.

Jill McDonough

The true experiment of Henry David Thoreau's *Walden* may be how it offers itself to continued experimentation. In *Proverbs of Earth*, through a two-year process of disassembling and reassembling Thoreau's language, Lance Newman affirms *Walden's* enduring values for a deeply lived life amid the chaos of 21st-century capitalism. In the New West and a century plus later, Newman faces the "harlequin art of poetry" that "serves up quaint routines of acid and fire" to configure beautifully resonant and humble "broken proverbs" that extend Thoreau's quest to find transformation between a content life and a life of "fire."

Marcella Durand

Lance Newman's *Proverbs of Earth* speak from a crossroads where the past meets the future in an unrealized present in which much is at stake. In these sometimes direct, sometimes oblique, always tight and understated constructions of insight and implication, a historically-rich reverence for the physical earth ties directly into contemporary ironies and dangers. Rather than violating their surroundings through new stages of turmoil indifferent to anything but itself, the poems and their tentative wisdom explore the all-too-human problem of how to create, and recreate, a consciousness that might be connected to the world in which it finds itself. These are proverbs for right now, and we need them.

Mark Wallace

In *Proverbs of Earth*, Lance Newman squeezes fresh insights from a vaunted lexicon, itself deliberately alive. Read as a whole, these "cellared words" explore Thoreau's themes from new and artful angles: our fraught systems of labor, tensions between humans and nature, time's irrepressible tide. But the true pleasure of Newman's collection is encountering its jewel-like poems as meditations whose wisdom accrues. These pieces turn artfully and unexpectedly—masterfully couple sound and sense—and remind us that we, like "all animals / combust for a time".

John Miller

Proverbs of Earth
Lance Newman

SPUYTEN DUYVIL

New York City

ISBN 978-1-963908-57-2

Library of Congress Control Number: 2024952288

For Ron Briley

"Eternity is in love with the productions of time."

—William Blake, *Proverbs of Hell*

I stretch my life to fit
then come to see others
as kin in tight coats.
Phrases gather like dried
birds. I finger plain truths
that cannot clothe me.

Prudence loads a tenement
with bread to show how far
we've pressed our lives into thought.
The good dwell in their labor
on one condition: the pages
fray. Our bodies slump and slew
as awake as fire in fields.

Eyes born of soil cleanse the fields
of graves. When I shovel up
cracked heads and saw-scarred bones
I rhyme the past and compost.
The dead feed me a thin
gruel of planks and spars
under a ceiling of years.

I mistook time for the cracked
rhymes moths chewed into my books.
The fruits I eat now were once
out of my knowledge.
Art settles to earth. Lives come
and go in play and pain.

My headlights pick out
a shovel in the grass.
There is no honest way
to recall which truths
I trusted once. Echoes
prove that thinking too
can pass for silence.

I measure valleys
by the oaks they grow
and peaks by the furrows
they plow into the clouds.
Water and land look
so immortal against
a horizon of fire.

Watch how time crimps
the sallow art of commerce.
Old vines bear split fruit.
The stances and voices
we collect strand us
like silent neighbors.

Mountains fuel the inner heat
that clothes can only hold
and prairie grass breathes
by sheltering vermin.
These eat less. Those sweat more.
But all animals
combust for a time.

Disease draws the body
like a draft pulls fire.
The only surprise is that
shivers stop before the mind.
Tell how you've prepared
to harbor in the land.

When lovers are fettered
by the dross of rules,
the heat of small lives
will keep the nest clean.
When blooms and fruit fail
scour the galls for worms.

The heavens sheathe the earth.
Soil clothes the mesh of roots.
Selfless fire rises in the duff.
Some bellies swell with famine
while others bloat with child.
How does my raw talk
become knowledge?

Doubt rises from doubt
and stirs me to my work.
In shaky moments
sick with prayer trust
the disease. Its nature
is to be incurable.

The wind sluicing down slope
dissolves my intelligence
but time is voluntary
in obscure weather.
The town in winter
may sink into a hilltop.

I can cheaply acquire
a sense of fellowship
in a routine transaction
with a scatter of stones
but can I weave a basket
to carry a new word home?

Ice buckles on the cobbles.
I trade offers with the tide.
A vessel of errors drives
west on the wind and reaches
the market at nightfall.
Truth is as constant as work.

Majestic horses give way
to the novelty of engines.
Queens must still undertake
wooden loves every day
but a hound can invest in
a rustic coat of culture.

My house imports flat light
and exports the glow of loss.
I could yield a little heat
if you draped today in grace.
Travel happens when
a raw span of time
joins the world to itself.

I respect the accidents
that unravel a green
country at its edges.
Weathered legs carry
the shiftless to good
company at last.

Accidental farms
will last until people
silence their desires.
A lost coat manifests
as a broken crow
until the light shifts.

Thieves travel a gentle
road to wealth and respect.
Slough the muck and don
a glossy suit of skin.
Who knew an old bottle
could sail the farthest pond?

Be ready for friends
clad in integers
and stripped of the green
bark of thought. What
follows from what I know?
Even ordinary talk
wears at the creases.

People priced my mind
and bought my entrails
as cheap as the hollow door
they opened to usher me
back home. In parables
snow was clothing enough.

My face isn't as grave
when I tailor snug answers
to questions I never thought
to ask. An oracle
quoted me to myself.
What we use is true.

The grace of maggots
hatched in a sailor's
legs reminds me I've
forgotten a charade
I played once and lost.
Laughter holds its shoulders
as slack as a shipwreck.

I worship my eyes
like holy monkeys
but I've glassed in my mind.
The harlequin art
of poetry serves up quaint
routines of acid and fire.

Another soldier learns
that a lie requires
a ready believer.
People hang their laughs
on pegs like caps and gowns.
Will we keep to the fierce
logic of custom and trade?

Families shake old letters
to find out which whims figure
now in the red threads
of accident. Language
evolves like coats and cars.
I once wished to speak
as plainly as a riot.

When I extinguish myself
winter seeks the usual
windows. The first painting
was made to suit simple wants.
A fragile skin of symbols
stands proud on the margin.

Doves dwell under
a roof of grass.
The sun finds dignity
in the slightest desire.
There is still some air
to cherish for a time.

A child on the hearth
of a singing cave. A life
played out in the distance.
If I survive the stars
spinning through the palms,
innocence will look
as easy as sleep.

My house shelves me
like an unread book.
Outside, bodies creep
to shelter in a cash
market for longing.
Birds know a fenced mare is
the mother of a meadow.

I keep a museum
of jobs in case the town
asks if a tent in the wind
is liberty or alms.
Even a ruptured crypt
still holds a few live songs.

Say boxes of bodies
carpet the hallways
and I get up a book
of dollars and death
that uses metaphors
mostly for effect.

When flakes of warm light
auger through the leaves
I amble over to see
who has raised a roof
against the coming rain.
Fire adorns my memory
with the cinders of loss.

In a house of live-edge slabs
I screw down every lid
and line the jars in ranks.
Work is hardly the worst
waste of hours and hands.
Air makes a fine subject
when I appear to write.

I salvage odd scraps
like a tight landlord
and hang every door
to close by its weight.
When a shadow slips in
I feel the weight in the dark.

The littlest numbers
tax my attention most.
I live by formulas
just to scavenge
a second-hand nest.
Dollars can't compare to chairs.

Freedom reaches its half
life in a dark basement
full of pipes and wires.
A house is a garment
that hires you to wash
and wear it for a time.

I gulp time like water
to still the clatter of sleep.
If I am a script
the show will play well enough.
I will invent heaven
as I come to it.

Funerals help arid
fathers picture a future
where the graves ring with order.
The worst damage comes
when my neighbor rejects
the truth of music itself.

My friends clog our talk
like machines of doubt.
They mortgage their minds
until their shoulders
stiffen into history.
The slightest exchange taxes
what I know of my ideas.

I do respect the lies
of property and freedom
but some common chores
like sanding a plank
make me confuse
gloss with precision.

The earth speculates
in fences and grass.
A village is a snare
for families and livestock.
My reason skips a beat
when a broken proverb
weighs me down with trust.

Bodies grow in shanties
like winter garlic.
We bury the poor
under cinder blocks
and mossy shingles.
The usual creatures
walk among the tombs.

When my legs traverse old maps
they confine me to names
marked down by the state.
Messengers carry the crown
of youth without complaint.
Who operates my mind
when my eyes are at sea?

My skin glows like a gift
but I think I'll sew a coat
that's suited to the grave.
Minds gradually put on
more comfortable beliefs
until shoes become the rule.

Trains and pubs made the empire
then dust and desks followed suit
sporting a halo of tunes.
When the present blows over
I'll gather mercies from grass
and follow a herd of stars.

All the modern clutter
of safety assumes I'll hum
away my days in a house
but hunger finds refuge
in the free flow of breath.
The mountains are naked
and age gave them their names.

One way to lie is to live
for trinkets in the cellar.
The savor of a good
question bolsters the facts.
There's no shelter like
the certainty of wind.

The mountain blessed my field
with sediment so I built
a family under the pines.
We adapted to the green
years before the land
grew as dry as a lord.

In my haste to be clay
wit wore longer than skin.
A still spirit cut
a path through my wants
and an echo took root
in the pale life I outgrew.

In a city of tents
well-made shingles still shed
more rain than blessings.
A lark swells on a red hedge.
Families adopt mansions
where culture is work not art.

A pond is a space looking
at itself striped with thaw.
Standing timber dissolves
in the disturbed plane.
The present gropes through
another hour. Numb bodies
cackle. The spring of reason.

A hickory of crows
gapes at a torpid snake.
I'll hew to the margins
where trees and wind cross paths.
My neighbor's lamplight
calls me to my work.

A heap of compost.
The fragrance of wings.
The sound of tendons.
Art saws open an oak
floor and finds butter
wrapped in a jacket.

Serene scavengers mulch
last year's saplings and dropped nails.
Just one trilling thrush
might warp my neighbor's fence
until the staples pop.
Carpenters of music
measure chance on the bench.

I could have kept the profits
to myself when time carted
the sun over the mountain
but why waste treachery?
A window is worth
more than a door.

Time trusts roots well sunk in sand.
The sun warms pines in order.
A shimmering black feather
lofts into shelving light.
Life lies at the bottom
of a thawing marsh
as open as an eye.

I'd rather borrow a stone
than burrow through roots
and dent my character.
I may only ever record
one or two genuine facts:
a watch in the flue,
a loaf on the pond.

I think in scraps of fire
at fixed hours. Birds commuting
to set down a clutch of eggs
just there. The theatre
of baking in a storm.
I once thought nobility
might live on the next block.

Honesty fits us
for labor so we preach
nests to chattering squirrels.
Destiny is just
an idea like sugar.
Does the universe ever
doubt its own desires?

Even a barnacle
is architectural,
a cone of common truth
seeded on a cornice
and grown fast as a fact.
Switch the ornaments
and the foundation.

In another timid sketch
of green olives a painter
sees the end of virtue.
The maker of dirt knows
which coffin fits their despair
but can color occupy
the shell of awareness?

One life is a snare
and one a winter cottage.
Indifferent rain taps the flue.
A window is the better
altar. The plumes of a gale
give way to a breeze of truth.

I tenant a plain box
of shingles daubed with sap.
A squatter wishes for silence
and a shed full of timbers,
but we can agree to speak
of a formula for loss.

One person pretends to sing
while another says music
is futile. Games, art, talk, thought,
they all need oversight,
but rules set the scene for fraud.
The drone of science infects
play with selfish conjecture.

Students orbit truth
like vagabond moons
or motes in a swarm.
They navigate the harbor
of thought by satellite
and devour facts through toys:
microscope, telescope, eye.

Sometimes I peck at a poem
like a telegraph tapping
cash into the distance.
Can I tell this day from that
when the honey travels
so many miles to my cup.

My first job earned my way
to a place as notional
as stocks and bonds.
I'd like to take a real rest
from the hard wind of money
and core my hours like apples.

I dream of hickories
but my lot is all in pines.
A smarter farmer would
sell their water but I grow
answers between the stumps
and trade wishes for time.

A bushel of transient
souls grew in a meadow
where I spaded in a row
of corn as sweet as belief.
All the dollars ever
floated will return to ground.

I speak animal
memories in public,
the same week after week.
The idle pray for work.
Peace is a lie that plays
to the ruins of insight.

Children in printed rags squint
through fixed sights at enemies
they bought off the shelf.
A nation of headstones knows
little and remembers less.
Shrines show the public its mind.

Stonecutters harvest hills
to entomb the young
but some bedrock is alive
enough to grow garlic
for the world's kettles.
Faith springs from the rod
then promises butter.

Dogs give way at last
to temples and bombs.
Up go the shouts
and accidents of thought.
Given time, we all make
the same excuses for love.

The sweet musk of slaughter
may mend the guilt I mouth
as little messes migrate
from dresser to closet.
Sharp tools afford the butcher
joy and balance his accounts.

Can I trust water after
a long week of nothing
but bread and statistics?
I yield to trivial sweets
like mild weather when what I
want is the salt of knowledge.

The ferment of devotion
demands that I bake my bread
on a saw blade. The spirit
may go to seed but wild yeast
will yield by and by
to the business of faith.

Sometimes decay invents
vital rites. Gentle souls steep
and swell on a day that sours
at the speed of eggs and meat.
No idea ever makes
enough time for the law.

When I bake bread I omit
kneading and leaven the dough
with a purse full of words.
I drink from a walnut shell
and take shelter from the sun
under maples in color.

I salt my cuffs and barter
hard for a frayed acre,
a short bushel of plums,
and my father's frayed jacket.
I'm workshy as cold
molasses in the jug.

Skeptics stack their feet
on heaven's firedogs
where skillets of roots
smoke like philosophy.
Oil rises in the wick
to light the board where
I write my questions.

The poor buckle and gnaw
at the rose of freedom.
My oldest acquaintances
quiver like empty bags.
Faith needs furniture.
Looking glass. Washbowl. Chair.

A spider litters the yard
with dry carcasses. I close
a shutter on the newly
burnt fields. Let's pretend
the dead pass through a knothole
to meet their missing friends.

I collected a bundle
of moons in a trunk. Pity
the conviction that fades
under a meat-red sun.
Inward flames provoke me
to rub my days to a high shine.
Nothing can find its way.

Instead of dust I gather
the fables nations tell
to celebrate their tools.
Clothes piled for a fire
then a tottering retreat
across patchy sod.

My fathers auctioned off
their husks and dross for rest.
I keep a fire of ideas
and gorge myself on trust.
My appetite for new
beliefs may be medicine
when doubt is my sacrament.

I crush herbs and savor
curses that call to mind
the little years when I proved
I'm wise enough for work.
My most outward sign
of grace is singing poems
in chorus with the wind.

I've cellared my fugitive
doubts so I can neighbor
with you in the commons.
The pastime of silence
is free. I won't trade folded
hands for the noise of means.

Good manners taint meat
and gifts confer duties.
Our first is to join
thoughts separated by time
and cover the walls with truths.
I veer from a path of stars
to the simplest of jobs.

To sacrifice pleasure
for wisdom may yield
spare time at the wheel
but I don't trust myself
to find my fellow vagrants.
I try to be content
but I'd rather preach fire.

The moon kindles good work
and words. I aim to be
and seem in common with
the wind when it mingles
its song with a dog's howl.
I freeze at the bright
certainty of his death.

The kind of birth that scorches
heaven hurled me headlong
into speech. How can I
love crusaders who help
by accident or forgive water
that torments raw earth?

What is spring in a year when
viral dust sifts down the ditch?
Should I thunder or choke
on the carrion smell of raw thought?
I balk at the usual forms
of suffering for money.

Some people believe spending
on the lie of balm is wrong
but peace may mean striking
a false bargain for shirts.
Property thanks the poor
and boasts of quiet virtues.

The breath of plants hides
the contagion's sympathy
with pain and floats me to rest.
Memory casts off disease
but the bloom of despair
shadows my foresight.

I believe in gnawing
on the ripe enormity
of a private morning.
Even abstractions
seek glory in rest.
Some justice is as plain
as the taste of a plum.

I sprung from a thicket
where lichen spots the maples.
I try to speak freely
but my manners echo
the stumbling rhythm of fear
in the first blush of distress.

An unripe apology
pains the wounded. I'd never
promise to rescue my friend
from sinking in waves. Cracked
memories of rain soothe me
when I draw from a dry well.

Whatever saints and states
say about the power of hymns
no sympathy with trees
can surpass their transience.
A shriveled cypress shows
prophets can publish truth.

When I feel too holy
I dream of windfall apples
and savor cellared words.
A farm is a gathering
of lifetimes on the land
and truth sprouts in fallow fields.

I walked miles to the market
stall where I bought the deed
to a season of eyes.
My crops improved when I learned
better than to mortgage
my work to a broker's taste.

I grow the sort of oaks
that live in the derelict
undergrowth of hours.
They drop the seeds of a time
that may be on your mind.
What if we refused
to burn dollars for fuel?

Suppose the milk of retirement
separates in the field.
I refuse to tally
my assets but I keep
a wheelbarrow to carry
my mind to the woodlot.

The young will collapse
in the intervals of fog.
A tree gnawed by apple moths
rhymes with the ruined barn
concealed in the hollow
where I grub for color.

A garden looks for a mind
that can afford to rest.
Every crease in the soil
strains my thin knowledge.
The earth roosts in dew
and we write what we hear.

Nonsense turns on rustic
greed for the things we jail.
The land is low enough now
to flood and float me
into a final mirage.
The pain of an excuse
buries the seeds of grief.

My neighbor cut a window
to light what will be her room.
The timbers and glass
will abide when she dies
and this page will still read true
where it shims the frame square.

I navigate the harbor
by accidents of recall.
Hand-hewn planks drift by seawalls
scrubbed white by summer's wake.
I'll trade you my stock of time
for the sand of empire.

A dry orchard clothed
in red birds reveals a song
at rest in a cage of roots.
The air near shore impresses
ripples on a known skyline.
The lake leads south by degrees.

I dwell with the builder
of shorebirds between a stream
in flood and the setting sun.
When I phantom above
a continent of clouds
lakes form in the valleys
like coins tossed at heaven.

Only a planet's dry crust
can foresee a distant age
when astronomers will live
near a meadow's locked gate
and dream of a plateau
high above the seething sea.

When I squinted across
the fence at history
a clamor of stars stretched
west to an oak confined
to a pasture in full view
of a packed universe.

Feed me a season of rest
on a pale morning. I am
as sincere as a trumpet
bathed in the part of now
that will last forever.
The hour before dawn frees me
to say what I will forget.

Markets creak like icy buoys.
Flocks of finches wheel and sing.
Nature is all buzz and hum
and hours of scrubbing
brushes. Am I equal to
an awakened life?

If I crawl through a sunlit
window some everlasting
star will see that a fact
takes extra effort when faith
infects my knees and eyes.
I perform my beliefs
in the corners of my life.

I fell asleep in the damp
air of memory and art.
What music will wake me?
The fragrance of despair?
The drowsy wisdom of clocks?
Poems or bells at dawn?

I'm trying to learn the art
of awareness by sketching
a study of my hopes.
My mechanical desires.
Swaths of ordinary facts.
A picture of how and why.

Is it petty to allow
the sea to tip and founder
while I trace the whorls
on my dying fingertips?
Extremes create their own
wretched forms of virtue.

Sand can be a cool bed
in season but sound sleepers
know commerce aims to trap
their dreams of a border
that's forever reckoning
with the bare fact of sunlight.

I devote sleep to laying
rails across the years and I
never wake to my own work.
The hue of night can gladden
an hour of doubt, but there's no
way to know why we talk
about the sound of ice.

The purpose of an eye
may be to find and follow
a child who wakes up knowing
what to do with the hours
we see in a bell and flames.
On the outskirts of time
I pray and pocket a seed.

My paper desires thunder
when I sit to a crop
of poems like tasseled ears
preaching a sudden turn.
Snow never needs the pressure
of ideas. Can the vessel
of thought stay true to winter?

I'm a lucid ruin
killing another year,
a memory of a paper
state that murders wit.
When infants read the news
the throng fails together.

The voice of history
bellows marches and sermons.
I was once drowsy enough
to believe dignity
is the sublime self-deceit
of hunting for routine.

When I untangle my thoughts
new fallacies shadow
my longing for old stories.
I try to ask questions
without guessing the answers.
Would I know a forest
that saw me as a father?

If I never whistled
at the pieces of a snapped
mast, a tick in a nutshell
might upset in the whirlpool.
The shallows rustle in time
with answers knocked from a bell.

It takes fire to cleave a state
from the sediment of time.
The rising flood of belief
wedges facts in the current.
An alphabet takes root
in the wisdom of sand.

The frost of ages lets
children fast on the outskirts
of a moment drenched in art.
I've learned to divine
the marrow of mind
in the sweet slush of time.

I crave the rattle of sun
lighting a rift in the wall.
Can I grasp a universe
that's true to ringing hills?
Fair is as fair sees
and it all ends in music.

LANCE NEWMAN's poems have appeared in many print and web magazines in the US, UK, and Australia. He has published three chapbooks: *Come Kanab* (Dusie, 2007), *3by3by3* (Beard of Bees, 2010), and *Satellite View* (Finishing Line, 2025). *Proverbs of Earth* is his first full-length collection. Newman teaches literature, media, and writing at Westminster University in Salt Lake City, Utah.

lancenewman.org

www.ingramcontent.com/pod-product-compliance
Lightning Source LLC
Chambersburg PA
CBHW030512130626
46549CB00007B/2963